Pompom Noël

P9-DTO-504

NO LONGER PROPERTY OF
SEATTLE PUBLIC LIBRARY

SEP - - 2018

First published in 2018

Search Press Limited
Wellwood, North Farm Road,
Tunbridge Wells, Kent TN2 3DR

Pompom Noël uses material from the following books
in the Twenty to Make series by Alistair Macdonald:
Fabulous Pompoms (2015) and *Pompom Christmas*
(2015)

Text copyright © Alistair Macdonald, 2018

Photographs by © Paul Bricknell, Ruth Jenkinson
and Laura Forrester

Photographs and design copyright
© Search Press Ltd., 2018

All rights reserved. No part of this book, text,
photographs or illustrations may be reproduced
or transmitted in any form or by any means by print,
photoprint, microfilm, microfiche, photocopier, internet
or in any way known or as yet unknown, or stored in a
retrieval system, without written permission obtained
beforehand from Search Press.

Print ISBN: 978-1-78221-706-0
Ebook ISBN: 978-1-78126-632-8

The Publishers and author can accept no responsibility
for any consequences arising from the information,
advice or instructions given in this publication.

Readers are permitted to reproduce any of the items in
this book for their personal use, or for the purposes of
selling for charity, free of charge and without the prior
permission of the Publishers. Any use of the items for
commercial purposes is not permitted without the
prior permission of the Publishers.

Suppliers
If you have difficulty in obtaining any of the materials
and equipment mentioned in this book, then please
visit the Search Press website for details of suppliers:
www.searchpress.com

You are invited to visit the author's website:
www.houseofalistair.com

Printed in China through Asia Pacific Offset

Dedication

For our 'wee' pompom, TSM.

Pompom Noël

33 festive pompoms to make for Christmas

ALISTAIR MACDONALD

SEARCH PRESS

CONTENTS

INTRODUCTION

Pompoms have been used for centuries. In France and Belgium they were originally used to decorate naval uniforms, and in Italy they were sewn onto clergymen's hats – biretta – and to embellish the clothes of people celebrating in national dress. The word itself derives from the French word *pompon*, meaning 'ceremonial tassel'. More recent years have seen the pompom become a fashion statement; not just used to decorate hats or soft furnishings, they can be sculpted into wonderful shapes and transformed into something quite spectacular. Pompoms are a mainstay for many a crafter, but this book seeks to take them to another level altogether!

Christmas is very special for many people and it is great to create your own decorations to put up around the house, or to give as a gift to a loved one. There is nothing better than the satisfaction you get from making something yourself – something to be proud of.

This book covers a whole range of Christmas decorations and plenty of familiar Christmas characters too. Look inside to meet some of them: Rudolph with his red nose, Santa and Mrs Claus, a 'frosty' snowman and my personal favourite, a mischievous Scottie dog – well, I am Scottish!

All of the designs are easy to follow and come with step-by-step instructions, using either the traditional cardboard ring method of making pompoms, or the more modern plastic pompom makers that clip together. 'Pompom-ing' really is easy and I hope the projects in this book spur you on to incorporate this popular craft into your own Christmas.

Now, pick up your yarn, makers at the ready – let's continue this pompom revolution!

TECHNIQUES

Making pompoms with a plastic pompom maker

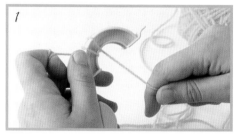

1 Wind the yarn round one half of the pompom maker.

2 Continue winding until you have created a thick layer, then start winding yarn round the other half.

3 When finished, close the pompom maker and cut through all the yarn.

4 Wind a length of yarn two or three times round the middle of the pompom maker. Pull tight and knot securely.

5 Release the pompom from the pompom maker and trim into a neat ball.

Making pompoms the traditional way

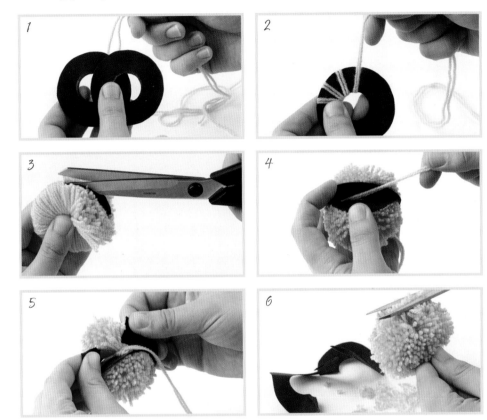

1 Cut out two identical cardboard discs to the diameter of the intended pompom. Mark out a smaller circle in the centre of each disc. This will form a hole to allow yarn to be passed through. As a rule of thumb, this circle should be half the diameter of the outer circle. Cut out the inner circles.

2 Hold the two cardboard discs together and start to wind your chosen yarn through the centre hole and around the rings. Cover the ring entirely until the hole in the centre has almost disappeared.

3 With fabric scissors, cut through the yarn between the cardboard discs round the outer edge. Cut round the entire circumference, releasing all of the yarn and revealing the cardboard discs.

4 Tie a spare piece of yarn between the discs to secure the middle of the pompom.

5 Once knotted securely, tear the cardboard to release the pompom.

6 Finish by trimming the pompom into a neat ball.

PROJECTS

I used a plastic pompom maker to make the projects in this book, in the following sizes: 25mm (1in), 35mm (1⅜in), 45mm (1¾in), 65mm (2⅝in) 85mm (3⅜in) and 115mm (4½in). However, you can also make the projects using the traditional method involving cardboard discs – simply cut them to the diameters above, and cut out an inner circle at the centre that is half the diameter of the disc.

I have used mostly inexpensive acrylic yarn, but remember that many of the projects require only small amounts, which you may already have in your yarn stash.

For all the projects in this book you will need fabric scissors and thread snips. Many of the projects also require a long, large-eyed sewing needle in order to thread ribbon through pompoms and attach pompoms to each other. Other tools required are listed on the project pages.

Some of the projects require templates. All templates are reproduced at actual size, so all you need to do is simply trace or photocopy them – easy! Please turn to pages 78–79 to see the full selection.

WARNING
If your pompom project is intended for a young child, please ensure all small parts, particularly eyes and buttons, are sewn or tied on securely. Projects with glued-on eyes are not suitable for children.

ROCKY ROBIN

Materials:

* 100g (3½oz) balls each of brown-flecked, light beige and burnt orange yarn
* Small amounts of orange and brown yarn
* 5 x chenille sticks, 30cm (11¾in) long
* 2 x black mounted sew-on gemstones
* Black sewing thread

Tools:

* Size 65mm (2⅝in) and 45mm (1¾in) pompom makers
* Small pliers
* Long, large-eyed sewing needle
* Regular sewing needle

Instructions:

1   Start by making Rocky's head and body. Open half of one of the pompom makers and wind on some burnt orange yarn. Fill one third of this half (decreasing to nothing as you meet the opposite side). Fill the remaining space with the light beige yarn. Fill the other half of the maker in the same way but use half as much orange yarn and swap the light beige for the brown-flecked yarn. Repeat the process with the other size pompom maker using the same colours. Trim each pompom into a neat ball. Attach the head to the body, sewing through both pompoms with yarn (see the photograph for positioning).

2   The legs, wings and beak are each made using the following method. One full chenille stick is required for the legs, one for each of the wings, plus a small piece for the beak. For the legs, wind a mixture of brown and orange yarn over a chenille stick to cover it completely. Then bend each end into a foot-like shape (see inset photograph opposite). Once you are happy with the shape created, close each foot by sewing the loose end to the rear of the foot, securing with a stitch. Bring the feet together to locate the middle of the chenille stick. Bend the middle section to form a shelf-like structure, running parallel with the base of the feet. This will give the body of the robin something to sit on. Position the body on to the feet and secure into position, sewing through the pompom body with yarn.

3   For the wings, find the centre of a chenille stick and wind the brown yarn round until you create a little mound of yarn in the centre. Bring the stick's ends together and continue to wind the yarn, encasing the sticks. Build the yarn up until you have the desired shape. Secure the yarn by sewing down at the smallest end. The beak is made using the same method as the wings, but with a smaller piece of chenille stick, about 4cm (1½in) long.

4   Hold the wings to the body to check the size. You can reduce the length of the wings by bending the smaller ends over if required. Wind some extra yarn round to hide the join and secure with another stitch. Once a pleasing shape has been achieved, sew the pieces directly onto the robin's body. Bend the wings into position.

5   To bring Rocky to life, sew the beak into position with yarn and the gemstone eyes with black sewing thread.

LAVENDER PILLOW STOCKING FILLERS

Materials:

- ❄ 2 x pieces of colourful cotton fabric per pillow, 10 x 15cm (4 x 6in)
- ❄ Small amounts of yarn in bright colours, to correspond or contrast with fabric
- ❄ Loose lavender
- ❄ Sewing thread

Tools:

- ❄ Tailor's chalk
- ❄ Size 25mm (1in) pompom maker
- ❄ Sewing machine
- ❄ Iron
- ❄ Ruler
- ❄ Knitting needle
- ❄ Sewing needle

Instructions:

1 Press fabric flat with a hot iron and, with right sides facing, pin to secure both layers.

2 Set a sewing machine to a medium-sized straight stitch and sew around the piece 1cm (½in) away from the raw edges. Make sure you leave an opening so you are able to turn through and fill with lavender.

3 Before you turn through to the right side, clip the corners and press the seam allowance along the opening side towards the centre. This will give you a nice crisp edge to sew up when you come to close the cushion. Turn through and tease out the corners using a knitting needle. Fill with lavender and slip stitch the opening closed.

4 Now make up four 25mm (1in) pompoms in your chosen yarn. Trim and shape into neat balls. Attach the pompoms to the four corners of the pillow with a needle and thread.

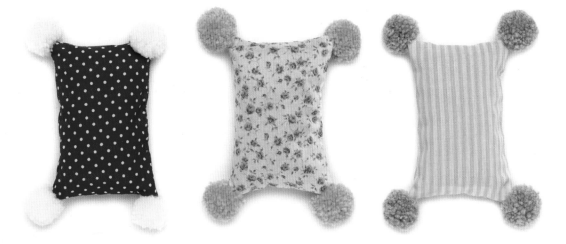

POMPOM BAUBLE

Materials:

❄ Small amounts of red, white and green yarn

❄ Scrap of red satin ribbon, 3mm (⅛in) wide

❄ Glass bauble of the desired size (I used one with a 90mm (3½in) diameter)

Tools:

❄ Size 25mm (1in) pompom maker

❄ Egg cup

❄ Pen

Instructions:

1 Remove the bauble top and place to one side. Sit the glass bauble on the egg cup to stop it from rolling away.

2 Make up two pompoms in each colour of yarn, so you have six in total. Trim each pompom into a neat ball.

3 Once you are happy that all six pompoms are of equal size and shaped carefully, insert them into the glass bauble. Use the top of a pen rather than your finger – glass baubles can break easily. A little pressure should be enough to push them through the neck of the bauble. Never use a metal instrument, as this may crack the glass.

4 To finish, carefully replace the bauble top and add some red ribbon to allow it to hang. Trim to the desired length and secure with a knot.

Try out different ideas for your bauble, such as using tinsel yarn. You could add more pompoms, or even stick rhinestones on to them.

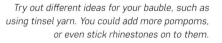

CUP AND BALL TOY

Materials:

❄ A4 (8⅓ x 11¾in) sheet of paper

❄ Small amounts of yarn in bright colours

❄ Red and white striped cotton fabric, 148 x 210mm (5⅞ x 8¼in)

❄ 2 x A4 (8⅓ x 11¾in) sheets of yellow felt

❄ Red satin ribbon, 3mm x 1m (⅛ x 39½in)

❄ Toy (polyester fiber) stuffing

❄ Sewing thread

❄ Fabric glue

Tools:

❄ Paper scissors

❄ Tailor's chalk

❄ Size 65mm (2½in) pompom maker

❄ Sewing machine

❄ Iron

❄ Sewing needle

❄ Compasses and pencil

❄ Ruler

❄ Knitting needle

❄ Pinking shears

❄ Pins

Instructions:

1 Start by drawing a template for the cone body. Set compasses to 9cm (3½in) and with an A4 (8⅓ x 11¾in) sheet of paper facing you in portrait position, place the pin of the compasses in the bottom left-hand corner. Draw a curve on to the paper. This will form the cone pattern. Cut out and place to one side.

2 Using the cone pattern, cut out two sections in yellow felt and one in a striped cotton. Place the two felt sections together followed by the striped cotton face down. Secure with pins. Set a sewing machine to a medium stitch and sew round the perimeter of the piece 5mm (¼in) away from the raw edge. Make sure you leave an opening to allow turning through. Clip the corners and turn right side out. Tease the corners out with a knitting needle and slip stitch the opening closed. With the cotton striped fabric facing you, topstitch around the entire piece 1cm (½in) from the edge with a sewing machine.

3 Roll the cone up, overlapping the top by 4cm (1½in). Pin to secure. Slip stitch with a needle and thread along the top of the cone and down the body until you reach the tip. Secure. Fill the cone with toy stuffing to about 7–8cm (2¾–3¼in) from the top. Cut a circle measuring 8cm (3¼in) in diameter from the yellow felt using pinking shears. Glue the circle into the cup to hide the toy stuffing.

4 Make up one 6.5cm (2½in) pompom in bright coloured yarn. After cutting but before removing the pompom maker, tie in the red satin ribbon. Remove the maker and trim the pompom into a neat shape, taking care to avoid the ribbon. Use the slack to attach to the cup with a needle and thread.

GARLAND

Materials:

❄ Small amounts of red, white and green yarn, or 100g (3½oz) balls each of red, white and green yarn if you are making a long garland

❄ Red double-sided ribbon, 3mm (⅛in) wide (this should measure the desired finished length of the garland)

Tools:

❄ Size 35mm (1⅜in) pompom maker

❄ Long, large-eyed sewing needle

Instructions:

1 Once you have decided on the desired finished length of the garland, you need to work out how many pompoms will be required. The simplest way to do this is to divide the length of the garland by the space between one pompom and the next. For example, if you wish to make a garland 2m (2¼yd) long, with a distance between each pompom centre of about 10cm (4in), you need to divide 200cm (78¾in) by 10cm (4in), which equates to 20 pompoms. Bear in mind that the longer you make your garland, the more yarn you will need.

2 Divide the number of pompoms you are going to make by the number of yarn colours you are using. In this case, we are using three colours of yarn. Always round the number up (better to have more pompoms than you need). Make up the required number of pompoms per colour, then trim each pompom into a neat ball using fabric scissors and place to one side.

3 Thread the red ribbon into the long, large-eyed sewing needle and start adding the pompoms to it. Do this gently to avoid pulling yarn out of the pompoms. Thread the pompoms on to the ribbon, alternating the colours and spacing them evenly. Continue until the length of ribbon is full.

4 Tie a small loop at each end of the garland to allow it to hang.

To make your garland different, you could try using a variety of pompom sizes.

CHRISTMAS TREE

Materials:

* 2 x 100g (3½oz) balls of green yarn in different shades (I have used a dark bottle green and a lighter racing green)
* Small amount of yellow yarn
* Small amounts of red and white/cream chunky yarn
* Piece of cardboard (parcel box cardboard is best)
* Scrap of green felt
* Green ribbon, 20mm wide x 2m (¾ x 79in) long
* Dry-cleaner's metal coat hanger

Tools:

* Paper scissors
* Size 115mm (4½in), 85mm (3⅜in), 65mm (2⅝in) and 35mm (1⅜in) pompom makers
* Glue gun
* Heavy duty wire cutters
* Pliers
* Compasses and pencil
* Long, large-eyed sewing needle

Instructions:

1 The tree body is made up of five pompoms. Make two pompoms using the 115mm (4½in) pompom maker and two using the 85mm (3⅜in) pompom maker. Make one pompom using the 65mm (2⅝in) maker. When making the pompoms, wind the dark green and the lighter green yarn onto the makers at the same time. This will mix the colours evenly. When the pompoms are made, set them to one side – do not trim at this stage. You need to keep a ragged-looking shape as this will help create a realistic tree effect.

2 Set the compasses to 5cm (2in). Mark out four circles on the cardboard and cut them out using paper scissors. These will be used to make a base for the tree to sit on. Now take a dry-cleaner's metal coat hanger and carefully cut the longest part of the frame free using wire cutters. Discard the rest of the hanger. Using a set of pliers, bend over a 25mm (1in) length from one of the tips to create an L-shaped piece of wire. To build the stand, glue three of the card circles one on top of the other. Find the centre of the fourth cardboard circle and pierce the wire through the centre. Glue this final circle to the other three, trapping the short length of the wire between the layers.

3 Disguise the cardboard rim by wrapping green ribbon round the base. Continue until the circumference is covered. Glue to secure. Wrap a second piece of ribbon round the base and tie a bow to secure. Trim the end to decorate. This will become the front of the tree. Set the compasses to 5.5cm (2¼in) and draw a circle on to some green felt. This is slightly bigger so that it hides the base. Cut out carefully and glue it to the base.

4 Assemble the tree body by threading the pompoms onto the wire. Start with the largest and end with the smallest at the top. Bend the remaining wire over at the top and conceal in the top pompom. You may need to trim the wire before bending. Make sure that all of the longer ragged ends on the pompoms are positioned on either side with the bow in the centre (see the photograph for guidance). Trim down the centre of the tree's body, both back and front, to neaten, but leave the ragged sides untouched.

5 For the star, make five pompoms using the 35mm (1⅜in) maker and the yellow yarn. Trim to form neat balls. Thread the five pompoms together to form a ring using leftover yarn and tie together to secure. Trim off the excess yarn. Before adding the star to the top, tie a length of red and white chunky yarn together and glue to the top of the tree. Twist the yarn along its length so that the colours alternate and coil it round the tree. Continue until you reach the base. Tuck the chunky yarn towards the underside of the tree and glue to secure.

6 Finish by sewing the star on to the top of the tree using some yellow yarn. Position the star to stand up proud. Stand back and admire your work!

HIS 'N' HERS GIFT TOPPERS

Materials:

❄ Small amounts of yarn in green (two shades) and pink

❄ Black grosgrain ribbon, 1.5cm wide x 1m (½ x 39½in) long

❄ White sewing thread

❄ Gift wrap with desired ribbons

❄ Cream dress net

❄ 2 x small toy cars

❄ Styrofoam balls, 1 x 2.5cm (1in) and 1 x 4cm (1½in) in diameter

❄ Scraps of thin pink ribbon

Tools:

❄ Size 25mm (1in), 35mm (1⅜in), 45mm (1¾in), 65mm (2½in) and 85mm (3⅜in) pompom makers

❄ Hand-sewing needles

❄ Glue gun

Instructions:

1 For the green gift topper, start by making the following sizes of pompoms: 1 x 85mm (3⅜in), 1 x 65mm (2½in), 1 x 45mm (1¾in) and 2 x 35mm (1⅜in). Make these in two different shades of green. Trim into neat balls. Wrap the black ribbon around three of the pompoms (the two largest and one of the smallest) to measure and cut an amount off for each pompom to form the road. Add the white road markings by stitching a simple, large running stitch with white thread along the centre of each ribbon. Attach the ribbon to the base of each pompom using a glue gun.

2 Wrap the gift with your desired paper and add ribbon if required. Arrange the hills and cars into position and secure them using the glue gun.

3 For the pink gift topper, use pink yarn to make the following sizes of pompoms: one 85mm (3⅜in) in diameter and two 45mm (1¾in) in diameter. Trim to neaten and place to one side (for these pompoms do not cut off the tied yarn as this will be used to secure them to the parcel). Cut out two squares of dress net on the double measuring 25 x 25cm (9¾ x 9¾in) and 15 x 15cm (6 x 6in). Wrap the dress net around the styrofoam balls and tie with the pink ribbon to encase each ball securely, leaving enough slack to form ties.

4 Wrap the gift with your desired paper and ribbon. Arrange the pompoms and encased balls into a design on top and tie into position using the ribbon tied around the parcel to anchor it. To finish, trim the excess ties to desired lengths.

RUDOLPH

Materials:

❄ 2 x 100g (3½oz) balls of brown yarn in different shades (I have used chocolate brown and mid-fawn)

❄ Small amounts of red and variegated brown yarn

❄ Scrap of brown felt

❄ 8 x chenille sticks, 30cm (11¾in) long

❄ Red ribbon, 1cm (⅜in) wide x 40cm (15¾in) long

❄ Small gold bell

❄ 2 x black sequins

❄ 2 x white highball buttons

❄ Fabric glue

Tools:

❄ Size 115mm (4½in), 85mm (3⅜in), 65mm (2⅝in), 45mm (1¾in), 35mm (1⅜in) and 25mm (1in) pompom makers

❄ Long, large-eyed sewing needle

Instructions:

1 Start by making Rudolph's head and body. These are made in the same way. Open half of the required pompom maker and wind on some of the fawn-coloured yarn. You are aiming to fill one-third of this half, decreasing to nothing as you meet the opposite side. Fill the remaining space with the chocolate brown yarn. Fill the other side in the same way, but this time use only the chocolate brown yarn. Repeat this process until you have completed three of the sizes required: one each of the 115mm (4½in), 85mm (3⅜in) and 65mm (2⅝in) makers. Remove the pompoms and trim into neat balls. Connect the pompoms, smallest to largest, with the two larger ones making up the body and the smallest one the head. Make the ears in the same way using the 35mm (1⅜in) maker.

2 Once the body is securely connected to the head, start to trim the surface of the pompoms until they blend together. The joins should fade into the next pompom seamlessly. You want to achieve a cone shape. Trim the bottom of the cone to create a flat base.

3 To make the snout, use the 45mm (1¾in) and 35mm (1⅜in) makers and some fawn-coloured yarn. Make a further pompom using red yarn and the 25mm (1in) maker. Connect the two fawn pompoms and trim into a cone shape as above. Trim the red pompom into a neat ball and attach to the top of the cone using spare yarn. Now position the snout and attach to the head. With the snout in place, sew the ears to either side of the head. Trim to blend the joins.

4 Each antler requires four full chenille sticks. Start by making a fold in each stick about 2.5cm (1in) down from one of the ends. Wind the variegated brown yarn at this folded point to create a little mound of yarn in the centre. With the mound complete, fold the chenille stick end parallel to the main body of the stick and continue to wind the yarn, encasing the folded end. Build the yarn up until you have covered the entire chenille stick. Secure the yarn by tying off. Repeat this process until you have completed three for each antler. With the two remaining chenille sticks, use the same process as above but create mounds at both ends.

5 Twist three of the covered chenille sticks together and bend the tips to create an antler shape. Bend the double-ended chenille stick in half and attach it just below the point where the three chenille sticks divide. Bend into position. Repeat this to create the second pair of antlers. Then twist the bases of the antlers together and disguise the join with matching yarn. Bend together into a V-shape and secure in place, using spare yarn and a needle, at the back of Rudolf's neck (see inset photograph above).

6 Sew on the eyes and cut out two semicircles for eyelids from scraps of brown felt. Glue them into position, covering half of the eyeball. Glue a black sequin to the centre of each eye. Thread a bell on to some red ribbon and tie it round Rudolph's neck, complete with a bow.

SANTA CLAUS

Materials:

❄ 100g (3½oz) balls each of red and white yarn

❄ Small amounts of red and beige chunky yarn

❄ 5 x chenille sticks, 30cm (11¾in) long

❄ Wooden ball, 5cm (2in) in diameter

❄ Gold craft wire, 20cm (7¾in) long

❄ Small toilet roll inner

Tools:

❄ Paper scissors

❄ Size 85mm (3⅜in) and 25mm (1in) pompom makers

❄ Long, large-eyed sewing needle

❄ Glue gun

❄ Black marker pen

❄ Pink blending pencil

Instructions:

1 Start by making a frame for the hat. Lay three chenille sticks across each other to form a star shape. Twist the sticks together and mould into a cone shape. Cut a 1cm (⅜in) section from the toilet roll inner (keep it as a ring) and attach the chenille stick ends, spacing them evenly round the circumference of the cardboard, by folding them under and round the card. Once secure, bend the cone shape over to make the base for the hat. Cover the entire shape with the chunky red yarn, concealing the card and sticks. Secure the yarn by gluing.

2 To make the rim of the hat, cover two chenille sticks in white yarn. Fold about 7.5cm (3in) of each end of the sticks into the centre so that they meet in the middle and flatten the sticks using your fingers. Then hold both sticks together lengthways and wind more white yarn around to encase them. Continue until you reach a desired thickness. Bend this piece round the base of the red hat and secure by stitching at the rear with spare white yarn.

3 Using the 85mm (3⅜in) pompom maker, make one pompom in red yarn. Using the 25mm (1in) maker, complete a second pompom in white yarn. Trim into neat balls using fabric scissors. Glue the wooden ball on to the top of the red pompom. Draw on the eyes and add some rosy cheeks using the pen and pencil. Glue the white pompom to the end of the hat.

4 The same method is used to construct both the beard and hair. Cut ten lengths of beige chunky yarn approximately 20cm (7¾in) long. Tie the yarn in the centre to combine and secure. Make a second bunch of yarn in the same way. Glue one bunch onto Santa's face to create a beard. The knot should face towards the wood to conceal it. Spread the yarn across the face, sticking it into position with some glue. Trim the beard into shape, using the photograph for guidance. Glue the second bunch to Santa's head, using the same method, to create the hair. Glue the hat onto the head and trim Santa's hair as desired. Sew a loop of red yarn on to the hat to allow it to hang.

5 The final touch is to construct a pair of spectacles. Take the craft wire and wrap it round a pen twice, about 5cm (2in) away from one of the ends. This will create one of the lenses. Leave a small gap and repeat the process to form the spectacles. Cut the wire 2.5cm (1in) away from each lens and bend inwards. Place the spectacles on to Santa's head and glue into position.

FESTIVE WREATH

Materials:

- ❄ 2 x 100g (3½oz) balls each of five different shades of green yarn
- ❄ Flat-backed styrofoam ring, 25cm (9¾in) in diameter
- ❄ Green cotton fabric, torn into 2cm (¾in) wide strips (you will need 3–4 strips depending on the length of the fabric)
- ❄ Double-sided red satin ribbon, approx. 5cm (2in) wide x 1.5m (59¼in) long
- ❄ Double-sided green satin ribbon, approx. 1cm (½in) wide x 60cm (23½in) long
- ❄ Green embroidery thread
- ❄ Circle of green, red or burgundy felt, 25cm (9¾in) in diameter
- ❄ Fabric glue

Tools:

- ❄ Size 85mm (3⅜in), 65mm (2⅝in) and 45mm (1¾in) pompom makers
- ❄ Long, large-eyed sewing needle
- ❄ Tailor's chalk

Instructions:

1 Make up about 50 pompoms across all the sizes and shades of green. Trim into neat balls and place to one side. To speed up the making process, you can double up the yarn and use two balls of wool at the same time. If you wind four strands of yarn at once, you will fill the pompom makers in no time.

2 Place the styrofoam ring on to the felt, flat side down, and mark round it with chalk. Remove the ring and add a 1cm (⅜in) seam allowance to the inner and outer lines. Cut out the felt using fabric scissors. This will form a backing to the finished wreath and hide the inner workings.

3 Cover the white ring in strips of green cotton. Wrap the pieces round the ring until you have concealed the white. Secure the ends of the strips by hand sewing onto the ring using green embroidery thread.

4 Now comes the fun part! Arrange the pompoms round the ring and work out a rough positioning. Mix all the sizes and colours to create depth and texture. When you are happy with the overall shape, attach the pompoms to the covered ring using the long, large-eyed sewing needle and green embroidery thread. Do not be afraid to sew directly through the ring itself. Continue until the ring is covered.

5 To finish, make a large bow from the red satin ribbon and tie it round the bottom of the ring. Trim the ends of the ribbon into a fork shape. Sew a loop of green satin ribbon to the rear at the top of the wreath to allow it to hang. Conceal the raw workings at the rear of the wreath by gluing the pre-cut felt to the back. Hang the wreath to your door and be the envy of your neighbours!

A flat-backed styrofoam ring is ideal for hanging against a flat surface, and makes a sturdy base for the pompoms.

FAIRY CROWN AND WAND

Materials:

❄ 100g (3½oz) balls each of white, pink and lilac yarn

❄ Plastic headband, 2.5cm (1in) thick

❄ Dry-cleaner's metal coat hanger

❄ Yellow satin ribbon, 3mm (⅛in) wide x approx. 5m (5½yd) long

❄ Slim garden cane

❄ Florist's wire

❄ White sewing thread

Tools:

❄ Tailor's chalk

❄ Size 25mm (1in) and 65mm (2½in) pompom makers

❄ Ruler

❄ Wire cutters

❄ Pointed tip pliers

❄ Pliers

❄ Permanent marker

❄ Knitting dolly (hand-cranked)

❄ Awl

❄ Sewing needle

Instructions:

1 Cut off the hooked part of the coat hanger, keeping your fingers well away whilst doing so. Mark the middle point of the longest side of the wire with a pen. Use this mark to bend the first point in the crown with pliers (so the pen mark will form the top of the middle peak). Straighten out the wire on either side of the original hanger shape and create the two other peaks to sit either side of the taller middle peak. All of the points along the base, including the cut ends, should run in a straight line. Gently shape this line into a horseshoe shape, to follow the curve of the headband.

2 Using a knitting dolly, make up around 6–7 metres (6½–7½yd) of braid using pink yarn. Thread the crown wire through the centre of the braid until completely hidden. Cut off the excess braid to use later. Now form two small loops on the cut ends of the wire with pliers to secure the wire frame to the headband. Make two small holes in the headband on either side with an awl, 5cm (2in) away from the tips, and equidistant from the sides. Secure the wire frame to the headband using strong florist's wire. Snip off excess wire and flatten off.

3 Divide the remaining braid in two. Stretch open one end and pull it over the headband tip to anchor it. Wrap the braid around the band to hide the plastic to halfway along the headband. Repeat this step on the other side. Hide the braid ends at the back of the headband once they meet, cutting off the excess, and secure with needle and thread. Make up nine 25mm (1in) pompoms in white and three in lilac yarn. Use to decorate and finish the crown.

4 Using both pink and lilac yarn, make one 65mm (2½in) pompom. Once you have cut through the yarn, secure the centre of the pompom in the usual manner, but do not remove the maker at this point. Take a small length of yellow ribbon and tie on smaller lengths (the knot should be in the centre of the smaller lengths). When this yellow ribbon looks fluffy enough, tie into the maker and pompom centre. Remove the maker and trim the pompom, taking care not to cut the ribbon.

5 Cover a small length of cane with the remaining braid and secure one end into the wand head made in step 4 with a needle and yarn. To finish, make a pink 25mm (1in) pompom and attach to the opposite end.

GIFT BOX EARRINGS

Materials:

❅ Small amount of red yarn

❅ 2 x lengths of green double-sided ribbon, 3mm (⅛in) wide x 30cm (11¾in) long

❅ 2 x gold earring posts

❅ 2 x fish-hook earring wires

Tools:

❅ Size 35mm (1⅛in) pompom maker

❅ Long-nosed pliers

Instructions:

1 Using the 35mm (1⅜in) pompom maker, make two pompoms in red yarn. Trim to make a flat surface anywhere on one of the pompoms. Do not go too deep to start. With the flat part in eye line, trim another side at a right angle. Turn this new levelled line to your eye line and continue trimming at right angles. Once you have four equal sides, trim the last remaining sides to form a cube. Trim carefully until you are happy with the size and shape. Repeat this process with the second pompom to produce a second identical cube.

2 Tie some green ribbon round each cube in the same way as you would round a large gift-wrapped present and finish by tying it into a small bow. Take your time with this step as it is rather fiddly.

3 Now thread the earring posts through the centre of each pompom, making sure that the tied bows are off centre and visible. See the photographs for positioning.

4 Use the long-nosed pliers to snip the posts 1cm (⅜in) away from the pompom. Use the ends of the pliers to create a loop at the end of the post and attach the fish hook earring wires. Close the loops to secure. Now it's party time!

These cute pompom earrings can be personalized very easily. Try using gold or silver ribbon, or even sparkly, metallic yarn to emphasize the festive feel!

CHRISTMAS CARD PEGS

Materials:

❄ Small amounts of red and white yarn

❄ Red double-sided satin ribbon, 1.5cm (½in) wide and your desired length

❄ Scraps of light and dark green felt

❄ 6 x wooden spring-loaded laundry pegs

❄ Craft paper or card

Tools:

❄ Paper scissors

❄ Size 25mm (1in) pompom maker

❄ Glue gun

❄ Pencil and tailor's chalk

❄ Scrap of card, for template

Instructions:

1 Start by deciding how long you wish the ribbon that will suspend and display your Christmas cards to be. Tie a knotted loop at either end to allow it to hang and place it to one side.

2 Decide on a number of pegs to make. For each peg, use either red or white yarn to determine the berry type.

3 Either trace or photocopy the holly leaf template on page 78 onto some craft paper or card, then cut it out using paper scissors. Use this template and tailor's chalk to mark out as many leaves on the scraps of felt as you require. As a ratio, I have used three leaves per peg and 2:1 per colour. Cut out all the leaves and place to one side.

4 To complete a berry, make a pompom using either red or white yarn and a 25mm (1in) pompom maker. Make two berries per peg. Trim the pompoms into neat balls and set aside.

5 Assemble each peg by layering three leaves, alternating the colours. Attach the leaves to the peg using the glue gun. At the same time, glue two berries together and then on to the holly leaves. See the photographs for guidance on positioning leaves and berries.

6 Complete this process until you have enough pegs, then hang your cards to dazzle your Christmas guests!

These pretty pegs are quick and easy to make – if the postman brings more cards than you anticipated, just make a few more!

ANGEL

Materials:

❉ 100g (3½oz) ball of white yarn

❉ Small amount of yellow yarn

❉ Small amount of beige/cream chunky yarn

❉ Wooden ball, 5cm (2in) in diameter

❉ Pre-wired hackle feathers in white

Tools:

❉ Size 85mm (3⅜in) and 25mm (1in) pompom makers

❉ Long, large-eyed sewing needle

❉ Glue gun

❉ Black pen

❉ Pink blending pencil

Instructions:

1 Using the 85mm (3⅜in) pompom maker, make one pompom in white yarn. Then, using the 25mm (1in) maker, make five pompoms in yellow. Trim into neat balls and place to one side. Glue the wooden ball on to the top of the white pompom. Draw on the eyes, mouth and rosy cheeks using the pen and pencil.

2 To construct the hair, cut ten lengths of beige chunky yarn approximately 20cm (7¾in) long. Tie the yarn in the centre to combine and secure. Glue the bunch of yarn on to the angel's head. The knot should face towards the wood to conceal it. Spread the yarn round the head, securing it in position with some glue. Trim the hair into shape, using the photographs for guidance.

3 To form the halo, thread the five yellow pompoms together using some spare yellow yarn. Tie the two yarn ends together to secure. Trim off the excess. Lightly glue the halo onto the top of the angel's head.

4 Finish by twisting together a bunch of pre-wired hackle feathers (about five per wing). Part the feathers to create a pair of wings. Sew them to the rear of the pompom body using spare white yarn. Tie to secure.

This charming angel can adorn your Christmas table or mantelpiece – if you attach some yarn to her halo, you could even hang her on your tree.

CHRISTMAS PUDDING

Materials:

❋ 100g (3½oz) balls each of brown and black yarn

❋ Small amount of red yarn

❋ Piece of white felt, 14 x 14cm (5½ x 5½in)

❋ 10 x pieces of green felt, 3 x 8cm (1¼ x 3¼in)

❋ Craft paper

Tools:

❋ Paper scissors

❋ Size 115mm (4½in) and 35mm (1⅜in) pompom makers

❋ Glue gun

❋ Tailor's chalk

❋ Scrap of card, for templates

Instructions:

1 To make this delicious Christmas pudding, use a 115mm (4½in) maker to make a pompom in brown and black yarn. Use a ratio of two brown to one of black. Wind the three yarns onto the maker at the same time for a consistent colour spread. Trim the pompom into a neat ball. To make the holly berries, make a further three pompoms in red yarn using a 35mm (1⅜in) maker and set aside.

2 Either trace or photocopy the icing template and the holly leaf template on page 78 onto some craft paper or card, then cut it out using paper scissors. Use tailor's chalk to mark out the icing shape onto white felt and the holly leaves onto green felt. Cut them out. Glue the icing on to the top of the pompom and secure the dribbles of icing with a tiny bit of glue near the ends.

3 Attach the holly leaves using the same method. Glue all ten leaves to the centre of the icing section, spacing them evenly round the pudding. Glue the three holly berries to the centre as the crowning glory.

4 To add a further bit of character, fold and arch some of the holly leaves up towards the berries and secure with a little glue. This will give some of the leaves a 3D effect. Bon appetit!

For templates see page 78.

NAPKIN TIES

Materials:

❄ 100g (3½oz) balls each of red, white and green yarn – this will make enough pompoms for at least eight napkin ties

❄ 8 x lengths of red double-sided satin ribbon, 5cm (2in) wide x approx. 60cm (23½in) long

Tools:

❄ Size 45mm (1¾in), 35cm (1⅜in) and 25mm (1in) pompom makers

❄ Glue gun

❄ Pin

Instructions:

1 First, decide on how many guests you are inviting for Christmas lunch, as this will determine how many napkin ties you require.

2 Per napkin tie, make up the following pompoms: one 45mm (1¾in) in white yarn, two 35mm (1⅜in) in red yarn and two 25mm (1in) in green yarn. Trim the pompoms into neat balls and set aside.

3 Cut a section of ribbon 60cm (23½in) long and fold in half. Using a pin, mark the centre of the length. Unfold and lay the ribbon flat. To assemble the pompoms, start by gluing the white pompom to the central marked point. Follow this by adding a red pompom to either side of the white one, then a green pompom to the side of the red pompoms. The pompoms should be symmetrical through the centre of the white pompom – white, red and green (see the photograph below).

4 Cut the ribbon ends in a diagonal fashion to complete the napkin ties.

These festive napkin ties look great with crisp, white table napkins, adding style to your Christmas table.

PARTY GLASS MARKERS

Materials:

❄ Small amounts of yarn in assorted colours

❄ Double-sided satin ribbons in assorted colours, each approx. 3mm (⅛in) wide x 25cm (9⅜in) long

❄ 2 x gold bells per marker, 1cm (⅜in) in diameter

Tools:

❄ Size 25mm (1in) pompom maker

❄ Long, large-eyed sewing needle

Instructions:

1 Make up as many pompoms in as many colours as you think you will need. Cut the corresponding number of ribbon lengths.

2 Trim the pompoms into neat balls and thread up a needle with a length of ribbon. Carefully thread the ribbon through the centre of the pompom and remove the ribbon from the needle. Do this gently to avoid pulling yarn out of the pompom.

3 Tie a bell securely on to each end of the ribbon. This will add some festive cheer and stop the pompom coming loose. Repeat the above process until you have made enough glass markers to go round.

You'll never lose track of your glass with these fun party glass markers!

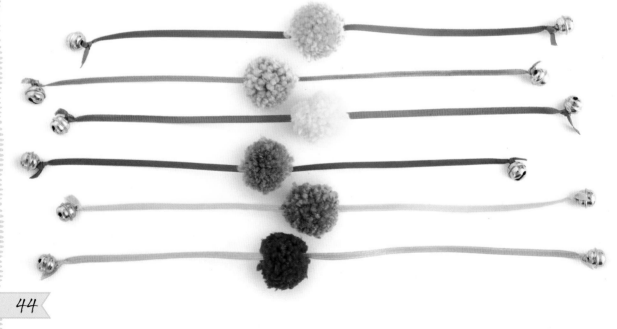

CHRISTMAS HEART

Materials:

* 100g (3½oz) ball of red yarn
* Dry-cleaner's wire coat hanger
* Red satin ribbon, 3mm (⅛in) wide x 1m (39½in) long

Tools:

* Size 25mm (1in) pompom maker
* Wire cutters
* Pliers
* Marker pen

Instructions:

1 Make up 33 pompoms using red yarn and a 25mm (1in) pompom maker. You may need more, depending on the size of your coat hanger when you have made it into the heart frame. Trim each pompom into a neat ball using fabric scissors and set aside.

2 To make the heart frame, first remove the hook top of the hanger with the wire cutters. Take care while doing this, keeping fingers well away when cutting. You will be left with a three-sided wire frame. Mark the middle of the long side with a pen. This is the first bending point. Using the pliers, bend the wire at the marked point, bringing the two shorter sides down to form the shape of a letter 'w'. The next stage is to begin to form the heart shape by straightening the hanger's existing curves with pliers. The hanger will now form the shape of an upside down 'v'.

3 Turn the 'v' so that it is the right way up, and mark 10cm (4in) along each side of the wire from the point of the 'v'. From these marks, begin bending the wire with the pliers to form the two lobes of the heart. When you are happy with the shape, bend a small loop at the tip of one of the cut ends.

4 Thread all of the pompoms on to the wire. You may have to tease them on. Make sure you go straight through the middles. Once they are all mounted, make a second small loop on the remaining cut end. Interlock this loop with the other one to secure the heart frame together. Push the pompoms towards the join to hide it.

5 Omitting the central pompom that covers the join, count four pompoms from the middle. Tie the red ribbon in between the fourth and fifth pompom on either side, then tie the ribbon ends together in a bow to form a hanger.

SNOWMAN GIFT TOPPER

Materials:

- ❅ 100g (3½oz) ball of white yarn
- ❅ White sewing thread
- ❅ Twigs from the garden
- ❅ 5 x small, horn-effect buttons (shirt button size)
- ❅ 2 x sequins
- ❅ Scrap of orange felt
- ❅ Wrapping paper and ribbon of your choice

Tools:

- ❅ Size 85mm (3⅜in), 65mm (2⅝in), 45mm (1¾in) and 35mm (1⅜in) pompom makers
- ❅ Long, large-eyed sewing needle
- ❅ Glue gun

Instructions:

1 Using the 85mm (3⅜in), 65mm (2⅝in) and 45mm (1¾in) pompom makers, make three pompoms, one in each size, in white yarn. Trim each of the three pompoms into neat balls. Join them together using spare white yarn and the long, large-eyed sewing needle. Begin with the largest and graduate to the smallest. Your snowman should be three-tiered.

2 Roll the scrap of orange felt up into a small cone shape and sew together using white sewing thread. This cone will form a nose and should measure about 3cm (1¼in) in length and 1cm (⅜in) in diameter. Glue the nose to the snowman's face.

3 Glue the sequins in place for the eyes and add the horn buttons vertically down the snowman's front. Trim the twigs into the desired shape and position them on either side of the body. Glue into position.

4 Make a further three pompoms using white yarn in the following sizes: 2 x 45mm (1¾in) and 1 x 35mm (1⅜in). These will decorate the surrounding area where the snowman is to sit. Trim into neat balls.

5 Wrap your gift in the paper of your choice and attach some ribbon. Do not tie a bow and keep the ribbon flat over the gift. You can hide the raw edges under the mounted snowman. Arrange the snowman and surrounding snowballs as shown in the photograph opposite. Use a glue gun to stick them down securely. Now for the other 59 presents!

The beauty of this snowman is that he will go with any colour or pattern of wrapping paper that you choose. Select a matching ribbon for the perfectly wrapped gift.

ELF CHRISTMAS STOCKING

Materials:

❄ 100g (3½oz) ball of white yarn

❄ Piece of red cotton fabric, approx. 100 x 112cm (39½ x 44in)

❄ Green double-sided satin ribbon, 5cm (2in) wide x approx. 1m (39½in) long (you can also use a thinner ribbon if you prefer)

❄ Green double-sided satin ribbon, 1.5cm (½in) wide x approx. 60cm (23½in) long

❄ Toy (polyester fiber) stuffing

❄ A3 (11¾ x 16½in) sheet of paper

❄ Sewing thread

Tools:

❄ Paper scissors

❄ Size 65mm (2⅝in), 45mm (1¾in) and 35mm (1⅜in) pompom makers

❄ Glue gun

❄ Pencil

❄ Tailor's chalk

❄ Sewing machine

❄ Pins

Instructions:

1 First, make a template for the elf stocking. On a sheet of A3 (11¾ x 16½in) paper, use a pencil to draw a freehand stocking shape with a curled pointy toe. You should fill as much of the space on the paper as you can. Cut round your lines. Do not add any seam allowance as there will be enough to take from this created pattern.

2 Use the template to mark out two stockings with tailor's chalk on to the red cotton fabric. Cut this out with the fabric doubled. One pair will form the outer stocking and the other a lining. Cut off the toe section from the lining pieces to aid turning through and stuffing.

3 Separate the two stocking fronts. With the right side facing you and the pointed toe to your left, lay out the wider green ribbon on to the red fabric. Space it evenly and in a diagonal direction and then pin to secure (see the photograph opposite for guidance). I have used three stripes; however, if you choose a thinner ribbon you could add additional stripes. Top stitch these pieces to the stocking using a sewing machine and a medium stitch length. Continue until all the sections have been completed. Remove the pins.

4 Separately pin the stocking outers and linings together with right sides facing. Machine stitch 1cm (⅜in) away from the raw edges, leaving the stocking open at the top. Repeat for the lining, but this time leave the stocking top and toe open. Once completed, bring together the rims of both the outer stocking and the lining. Pin together with right sides facing, taking care to match the side seams. Stitch together using a 1cm (⅜in) seam allowance. Clip into the curved lines and turn through. Feed the lining back into the stocking and top stitch along the rim, 5mm (¼in) from the edge. Stuff the toe with toy stuffing.

5 Along the rim find the centre back seam and add the 1.5cm (½in) wide green ribbon, which will act as a tie. To do this, fold the ribbon in half to find the centre and machine sew onto the outer part of the stocking. Trim the ribbon ends diagonally to neaten.

6 With the stocking completed, make up the following pompoms: two 65mm (2⅝in), 5 x 45mm (1¾in) and 1 x 35mm (1⅜in) in diameter. Trim into neat balls. Use a glue gun to attach seven pompoms randomly to the front of the stocking top and the smallest pompom to the pointed toe (see the photograph opposite for guidance). Then fill with goodies!

POMPOM TOTE TO GIVE

Materials:

- ❄ Assorted scraps of brightly coloured yarn
- ❄ Calico shopping bag, approx. 36cm (14¼in) wide x 42cm (16½in) long
- ❄ Sewing thread

Tools:

- ❄ Size 35mm (1⅜in) pompom maker
- ❄ Sewing needles or glue gun
- ❄ Pencil
- ❄ Ruler
- ❄ Paper

Instructions:

1 Start by making twenty-five pompoms with a size 35mm (1⅜in) pompom maker in assorted colours of yarn. Trim and shape all pompoms into neat balls.

2 With a pencil and ruler, mark out a grid on a sheet of paper. The grid should measure 30 x 30cm (11¾ x 11¾in). Divide each side by marking equal intervals of 6cm (2¼in). Join the marks up from left to right and top to bottom. You should now have a grid containing 25 boxes. Mark the centre of each square with a thick pencil dot. These will be used as placement dots for each of the pompoms.

3 Lay the grid pencil-side down on to the centre of the calico shopper and transfer the placement dots by going over them with the pencil from the wrong side. Arrange the pompoms on to the dots. Swap the pompoms around the grid until you are happy with the colour combination. Sew or glue them into position. Using a glue gun will give the pompoms a greater surface area on which to secure them.

GINGERBREAD MAN

Materials:

❄ 100g (3½oz) ball of gingerbread-coloured yarn

❄ Yellow 3D fabric paint

❄ White ribbon bow

❄ 2 x black sequins

❄ 3 x green buttons

❄ Red embroidery thread

❄ Fabric glue

Tools:

❄ Size 65mm (2⅝in), 45mm (1¾in) and 35mm (1⅜in) pompom makers

❄ Long, large-eyed sewing needle

Instructions:

1 Make the following pompoms using gingerbread-coloured yarn: one 65mm (2⅝in), one 45mm (1¾in) and six 35mm (1⅜in) in diameter. Trim the 65mm (2⅝in) and 45mm (1¾in) pompoms into neat balls. Connect the two together to form the body and head using a needle and some spare yarn. After joining, cut across the pompoms front and back to produce two level surfaces. This is to create a flatter, biscuit shape rather than a domed appearance.

2 Trim two of the 35mm (1⅜in) pompoms into neat balls. These are to form arms. Attach these to the body with a needle and some spare yarn. The remaining four pompoms will form the legs. Join two pompoms together with yarn and tie to secure. This will form a sausage-like shape. Level off one of the shorter ends and trim the other surfaces into a neat leg shape, blending the join. Repeat the process for the second leg.

3 Attach the legs to the body and secure with yarn. With the body as a guide, level the legs and arms in line with the rest of the gingerbread man. This will ensure a flat appearance. Add a loop of yarn through the head to allow it to hang.

4 Now for the fun part! Squeeze the yellow 3D paint round the perimeter in a wiggly line to replicate icing. Use fabric glue to add the sequin eyes, bow and buttons down the chest. Once the paint and glue have dried, give your gingerbread man a smile using some red embroidery thread and a needle. Make as many as you like, but don't eat too many!

CHRISTMAS CUPCAKES

Materials:

* 100g (3½oz) ball each of light brown and red yarn
* Small amount of yarn in a bright colour (I have used blue)
* Small amounts of white and yellow felt

Tools:

* Paper and pinking shears
* Tailor's chalk
* Size 25mm (1in) and 45mm (1¾in) pompom makers
* Pins
* Sewing needle
* Glue gun
* Scrap of card, for templates

Instructions:

1 Either trace or photocopy the icing and cake templates on page 79 onto a piece card, then cut them out using paper scissors. Set aside.

2 With red yarn, make up one 25mm (1in) pompom. This will form a cherry for the top of the cupcake. Using light brown yarn and a 45mm (1¾in) pompom maker, make a larger pompom. Trim and shape each one into a neat ball and set aside.

3 Lay the cupcake case template on to some yellow felt and mark out with chalk. With fabric scissors cut out the sides and base curve of the case. To create the serrated top of the case, carefully cut this top curve with pinking shears (shown by the zigzag red line on the template). Bring the short edges together, overlapping by about 4mm (⅛in), and pin to hold. Hand sew with a running stitch to secure in place, and remove the pin.

4 Take your small amount of brightly-coloured yarn and wrap it around the felt ring. Use the jagged tops as a guide. Leave two jagged points in between each line of yarn. Continue to wrap the yarn around the whole case until you reach the start. Tie both loose ends of yarn inside the case to secure. Trim the ends and rearrange evenly around the base of the case.

5 Cut out the icing shape using white felt. Sew the cherry to the middle to secure. Assemble the cupcake by glueing the brown pompom into the case, followed by the icing topper complete with cherry.

For templates see page 79.

MRS CLAUS

Materials:

❄ 100g (3½oz) ball of red yarn

❄ Small amount of beige/cream chunky yarn

❄ Small amount of green yarn

❄ 2 x red silk squares, 19 x 19cm (7½ x 7½in)

❄ Green cotton square, 17 x 17cm (6¾ x 6¾in)

❄ 3 x horn buttons (shirt button size)

❄ Wooden ball, 5cm (2in) in diameter

❄ Small scrap of green felt (optional)

❄ Sewing thread

Tools:

❄ Size 85mm (3⅜in) pompom maker

❄ Pins

❄ Glue gun

❄ Long, large-eyed sewing needle

❄ Sewing machine

❄ Compasses and tailor's chalk

❄ Black pen and pink blending pencil

Instructions:

1 Set the compasses to 9cm (3½in) and mark out a circle with a diameter of 18cm (7in) on to the red silk. Cut this out with the fabric doubled and pin with right sides facing. Machine stitch using a 1cm (⅜in) seam allowance and a medium stitch length round the circumference of the circle. Find the centre of one of the circles and cut an opening 2.5cm (1in) long with a pair of fabric scissors. Use this opening to pull the work through to the right side. Thread the green yarn onto the needle and add a running stitch round the circumference about 1.5cm (½in) away from the edge. Pull both ends of yarn, drawing the circle together to form the hat. Once you are happy with the shape, tie the yarn in a bow to secure and set to one side.

2 Make the shawl using the same method as the hat, but this time fold the cotton in half to create a triangle. Make a smaller opening to turn through, making this the underside of the shawl. Add a felt patch to hide if required.

3 Using the black pen and the pink blending pencil, draw the eyes, mouth and cheeks onto the wooden ball. With one continuous length of beige chunky yarn, add some hair to the head. Twist the yarn into loops to form curls and glue into position. Continue until you have covered the head.

4 Use the 85mm (3⅜in) pompom maker to make a pompom using red yarn and trim into a neat ball. This will form the body. To assemble, attach the body to the head with glue. Position the hat, shawl and horn buttons, again affixing with glue.

SNOWBALL WITH SANTA HAT

Materials:

❄ 100g (3½oz) ball of white yarn

❄ Red felt square, 15 x 15cm (6 x 6in)

❄ Red embroidery thread

❄ White sewing thread

Tools:

❄ Size 65mm (2⅝in) and 25mm (1in) pompom makers

❄ Glue gun

❄ Long, large-eyed sewing needle

❄ Regular sewing needle

❄ Compasses and tailor's chalk

Instructions:

1 Set the compasses to 7.5cm (3in), mark out a circle on to the red felt and cut out using fabric scissors. Fold the circle in half and roll into a cone. Once you are happy with the shape, hand stitch the cone closed along the straight edge using a needle and thread. I have used white thread as I want this to be visible to add some charm.

2 Make up one pompom of each size, 65mm (2⅝in) and 25mm (1in), using white yarn. Trim into neat balls.

3 Glue the hat on to the large snowball pompom and glue the small pompom to the tip of the cone. Bend the tip of the hat over slightly and secure into position with glue.

4 Sew a length of red embroidery thread to the top of the hat just below the pompom to allow it to hang.

You can make these sweet little decorations in any size. Why not make several hats using felt of different colours?

BAUBLE NAPKINS

Materials:

* Small amounts of yarn in your choice of colours
* Piece of cream cotton fabric for each napkin, 41 x 41cm (16¼ x 16¼in)
* Sewing thread

Tools:

* Tailor's chalk
* Size 25mm (1in) pompom maker
* Sewing machine
* Iron
* Ruler
* Sewing needle

Instructions:

1 Press the fabric flat with a hot iron. Set your sewing machine to a medium-sized straight stitch to hem the edges of the napkin.

2 You can either use a hemming foot or sew it by hand. Press 5mm (¼in) of fabric over along one edge of the napkin. Repeat this process on the same edge by folding over another 5mm (¼in), hiding the raw edge. Then either machine-sew the fold down, or sew it by hand.

3 Continue until all four sides are completed. Secure any loose threads and cut off the ends.

4 Make up as many pompoms as you require in lots of different bright colours. I have used sixteen in total, spaced around 9cm (3½in) apart. Once the pompoms are made, trim them into neat balls. You will need to make more if you wish the pompoms to sit closer together.

5 Ensure that you space the pompoms evenly. To help with this, attach a pompom to each corner and then to the middle of each side, and so on, until you have an even distribution.

SNOWFLAKE

Materials:

❄ 3 x 100g (3½oz) balls of white yarn

Tools:

❄ Size 85mm (3⅜in), 65mm (2⅝in), 45mm (1¾in) and 35mm (1⅜in) pompom makers

❄ Long, large-eyed sewing needle

Instructions:

1 Make up the following pompoms in white yarn: one 85mm (3⅜in), five 65mm (2⅝in), five 45mm (1¾in) and five 35mm (1⅜in). Trim into neat balls. To speed up the process, wind all three balls of wool onto the makers at the same time.

2 Measure out 30 x 3m (3¼yd) lengths of white yarn. Tie the lengths together at one end and divide into three groups of 10. Plait the yarn until you reach the ends. Secure with a knot.

3 To assemble, start with the largest pompom and place the five 65mm (2⅝in) pompoms around it in the circumference to create a flower-like shape. Now add a row of the plaited braid securing into the centre of each pompom using spare white yarn and a long needle. When you reach the centre of the pompom where you started, you will need to trim the braid. To do this, simply wrap and tie yarn round the point where you intend to cut. Tie a second section of yarn 1cm (⅜in) away from the first and then cut through the centre of both. This will stop the braid from coming undone.

4 Now add the 45mm (1¾in) pompoms and, as in step 3, a second layer of braid. Finally, add the 35mm (1⅜in) pompoms to the tips of the previous round of pompoms to finish. Attach a loop of yarn to one of the outer pompoms to allow the snowflake to hang.

This charming, fluffy snowflake is a little fiddly to put together, but it is a really simple project to make, and well worth the effort!

SCOTTIE DOG

Materials:

❄ 2 x 100g (3½oz) balls of black yarn

❄ Tartan wired ribbon, 5cm (2in) wide x 60cm (23½in) long

Tools:

❄ Size 115mm (4½in), 85mm (3⅜in), 65mm (2⅝in), 45mm (1¾in) and 35mm (1⅜in) pompom makers

❄ Long, large-eyed sewing needle

Instructions:

1 Start by making the following pompoms: two 115mm (4½in), one 85mm (3⅜in), one 65mm (2⅝in), four 45mm (1¾in) and two 35mm (1⅜in). Do not trim them at this stage. Attach the two 115mm (4½in) pompoms together using spare yarn and a needle. Make sure you line up the ragged edges of the pompoms. Place one of the ragged edges face down onto a work surface. Trim the top ragged edge to create the backbone of the Scottie dog. Only trim the immediate top and leave the rest of the yarn long, so that it appears fur-like. Set the body to one side.

2 Next, join together the 85mm (3⅜in) and 65mm (2⅝in) pompoms. These will form the neck and the head. Once they are securely connected, trim their surfaces until they blend together. One pompom should fade seamlessly into the next, with the join invisible. Aim to achieve a cone-like shape, leaving some of the yarn ragged at the top. Attach to the body, securing with yarn.

3 Join together the two 35mm (1⅜in) pompoms and shape as in step 2. Sew this on to the rear of the dog to form a 'waggly' tail. Trim two 45mm (1¾in) pompoms slightly, then sew them on to the rear of the head at either side to form ears, and the remaining two side by side on the front of the head to become the dog's snout. Trim into the desired shape, leaving these pompoms ragged for authenticity.

4 Tie a length of tartan ribbon round the neck, finishing in a plump bow. Trim the ribbon ends into a forked shape. As the ribbon is wired, you can manipulate the shape as you wish.

Why not make a white and a grey Scottie dog as well to keep this little chap company!

DOVE OF PEACE

Materials:

- 100g (3½oz) ball of white yarn
- Small amounts of brown yarn
- Small piece of chenille stick, brown
- White pre-wired feathers
- Scrap of red felt, approx. 7 x 3.75cm (2¾ x 1½in)
- White thread
- Blue mounted sew-on gemstones

Tools:

- Paper scissors
- Size 35mm (1⅜in) and 65mm (2½in) pompom makers
- Sewing needles
- Pointed tip pliers
- Tailor's chalk
- Scrap of card, for template

Instructions:

1 Either trace or photocopy the heart template on page 78 onto a spare piece of card and cut out with paper scissors. Pin it to the doubled red felt, and cut out the two heart shapes. Sew them together with a decorative running stitch, and set them to one side.

2 In the meantime, make one 35mm (1⅜in) pompom for the dove's head and one 65mm (2½in) pompom for the body in white yarn. Trim the smaller pompom into a neat ball and set aside. Instead of a ball, you will need to trim the larger pompom into an egg shape. Take your time doing this for better results – a little at a time. With the body completed, attach the head securely to one of the pointed ends with yarn.

3 Add some of the white feathers to form a tail. Push the wire through the body until it re-appears out of the other side. Trim the wire end and use the pointed pliers to bend it round and twist into the body, burying the wire out of sight. Finish the tail and use the same method when forming the wings. Keep adding feathers until you are happy with the look.

4 To form a beak, cut off a 3cm (1¼in) length of pipe cleaner and wrap the brown yarn around it. Bend it in half, bringing both ends together and wrap more yarn around the whole thing (do not make this too bulky). Secure the yarn and sew the beak into position.

5 Attach the sew-on gemstones as the dove's eyes to the head with a needle and thread. Then attach the heart to the beak with some white thread, making sure there is enough slack to allow it to hang.

WARNING
This item is not a toy – do not allow small children to play with it.

FESTIVE LANTERN

Materials:

❋ 100g (3½oz) ball of red yarn

❋ 2 x pieces of red felt, 6 x 6cm (2¼ x 2¼in)

❋ Yellow embroidery thread

❋ Florist's wire

❋ 2 x styrofoam rings, 9cm (3½in) in diameter

❋ Red satin ribbon 3mm x 1m (⅛ x 39½in)

❋ Battery-operated tea light (do not use a naked flame with your pompom lantern)

Tools:

❋ Tailor's chalk

❋ Size 25mm (1in) pompom maker

❋ Pointed tipped pliers

❋ Ruler

❋ Knitting doll (hand-cranked)

❋ Compasses

❋ Glue gun

❋ Paint brush and red paint (optional)

Instructions:

1 Make up twenty-five pompoms in red yarn with a 25mm (1in) pompom maker. Trim into neat balls and set aside. You will need five pompoms per arm of the lantern.

2 Use the rest of the red yarn to knit up 4 metres (4¼yd) of braid using a knitting dolly. If you use a hand-cranked version, this will knit up very quickly. Divide the braid in half. Use the braid to wrap round the styrofoam rings, hiding the white bits. When you have completely covered the ring, snip off the excess and secure with a glue gun. Tuck the loose ends under the wound braid to hide them. As an option, you could paint the styrofoam rings red first, so that you would not have to wrap the braid round so tightly to hide the white.

3 Hold one ring and insert a length of florist's wire from the bottom of the ring and out through the top. Pull the wire through, leaving a small section. Roll this section into a loop with a set of pointed pliers, flatten on to the ring base and hide it under the braid. Continue until you have five wires, equally spaced, to create arms.

4 Keep the wires straight and thread five pompoms on to each wire. Place the remaining ring on to the top of the wire tips and thread the ring on to all five. Push the ring down towards the pompoms. Snip the excess wire off just above the ring's surface and secure the ends as before (see step 3).

5 Set the compasses to 2.25cm (⅞in), mark a circle on some paper and cut out two circles in red felt. Glue the circles together and set aside.

6 Wrap a small amount of red yarn around four fingers and release the yarn by cutting underneath your little finger. Tie and secure the yarn in the middle. From this middle point, bring the loose ends together and tie the yarn near the top with yellow embroidery thread to create a tassel. Sew the tassel to the centre of the felt circle. Attach the felt circle into the middle of the base ring using a glue gun.

7 Now bend the arms into equal curved shapes and attach the red ribbon to the top to allow you to hang the lantern.

CHRISTMAS TEA LIGHT

Materials:

❋ 50g (1¾oz) ball of white yarn

❋ 3 x A4 (8⅓ x 11¾in) sheets of burgundy felt

❋ Scraps of felt in two shades of green

❋ 6 x gold jingle bells, 25mm (1in) in diameter

❋ Red satin ribbon, 3mm (⅛in) x 2m (2¼yd)

❋ One small glass with a 23cm (9in) circumference at the base

❋ Battery-operated tea light (optional)

Tools:

❋ Paper, size A4 (8⅓ x 11¾in)

❋ Paper scissors

❋ Tailor's chalk

❋ Size 25mm (1in) pompom maker

❋ Hand sewing needles

❋ Glue gun

❋ Ruler

❋ Compasses and pencil

Instructions:

1 Start by making your templates. Either trace or photocopy the mistletoe template on page 79 onto the A4 (8⅓ x 11¾in) sheet of paper, then cut it out using paper scissors. Set this aside. Now make your own template for the base of the tea light holder. Set compasses to 7cm (2¾in) wide and draw a circle on to leftover sheet of paper. Use the circle to mark out three base sections on to burgundy felt; this should use two sheets. Neatly cut out all three bases and layer together, securing with a glue gun. On the final sheet of burgundy felt, mark out a rectangle measuring 12 x 23cm (4¾ x 9in). Cut out and fold together lengthways, gluing to secure, and allow to dry.

2 With some chalk, mark a central line down the folded felt along the longest edge. Using fabric scissors, cut straight lines at 1cm (½in) intervals from the raw edge in towards the chalked line. Bring the short edges together and secure by sewing, but only down to the chalk line. This should form a cuff to grip the base of the glass. The raw edges should fan away from the glass. Placed the cuffed glass centrally onto the base section and glue the fanned rays to secure into place. Remove the glass so that you can decorate the holder.

3 Make up six 25mm (1in) pompoms in white yarn, trimmed into neat balls. Mark out as many mistletoe leaves in green felt as you require (I have used six per shade of green). Cut the ribbon into 30cm (11¾in) lengths and bunch together, securing at the base with a stitch.

4 Now all of your components are ready – pompoms, mistletoe leaves, sleigh bells and ribbon bunches – simply arrange and sew them on to the base. Try a few options first by pinning them down before you decide on a final composition. Please note that if you have a slightly wider bottomed glass, all you have to do is increase the length of the cuff and possibly enlarge the base section a little. Never use a real tea light without the glass.

TEDDY BEAR

Materials:

❈ 100g (3½oz) balls each of chocolate brown and caramel yarn

❈ 2 x mounted gemstones in black

❈ Black embroidery thread

❈ Scrap of black felt

Tools:

❈ Size 25mm (1in), 35mm (1⅜in), 45mm (1¾in) and 65mm (2½in) pompom makers

❈ Sewing needle

❈ Glue gun

Instructions:

1 Start by making the bear's ears, head and body. You will need to make two pompoms for the ears with the 25mm (1in) pompom maker, one 45mm (1¾in) for the head, and one 65mm (2½in) for the body. Open one half of the pompom maker and wind on the caramel yarn. Fill approximately two-thirds of this side with the caramel colour, and then fill the remaining third with the darker chocolate yarn, completing this half of your maker. Fill the empty side using only the chocolate colour.

2 Repeat this process until you have completed all sizes, then trim and shape the pompoms into neat balls. Attach the head to the body, and then the ears to the head, sewing through the pompoms with yarn for secure anchoring (see photograph for positioning).

3 The paws and feet are made using only the chocolate-coloured yarn. Make two pompoms for the paws with the 35mm (1⅜in) pompom maker, and two for the feet with the 45mm (1¾in) maker. Trim into neat balls and attach to the body. Position the feet to the front and the paws to the side.

4 Sew on the gemstone eyes and use black embroidery thread for the teddy's mouth. Cut a small black felt triangle to create a nose and glue it into position.

BERRY BROOCH AND EARRINGS

Materials:

❄ 50g (1¾oz) balls of red and green yarn

❄ Olive embroidery thread

❄ Sew-on brooch back

❄ 2 x earring hooks

Tools:

❄ Size 25mm (1in) and 35mm (1⅜in) pompom makers

❄ Sewing needle

❄ Knitting dolly (hand-cranked)

Instructions:

1 Each earring requires two 25mm (1in) pompoms in red yarn. The matching brooch requires two 35mm (1⅜in) pompoms. Make up the pompoms, then trim them into neat balls.

2 Using a knitting dolly (preferably a hand-cranked one for speed) make up 50cm (19¾in) of braid with the green yarn. Divide this into three sections. For the earrings cut the braid off at 10cm (4in), and 20cm (8in) for the brooch. Once the lengths are cut, finish the raw ends by sewing them closed with matching yarn. Sew a pompom securely on to the ends of the braid.

3 With the pompoms attached, fold the braid in half to locate the middle. Allow one side to be slightly longer to add character. About 1.5cm (½in) away from the middle point, join the braid together by wrapping embroidery thread around the work to create a band effect.

4 Attach an earring hook to the top of each loop with a needle and thread to finish the earrings.

5 Before attaching the backing to the brooch, slip stitch the braid together about 3cm (1¼in) at the rear to hold the braid closed and hide the metalwork. Then sew the brooch back to the rear of the piece.

TEMPLATES

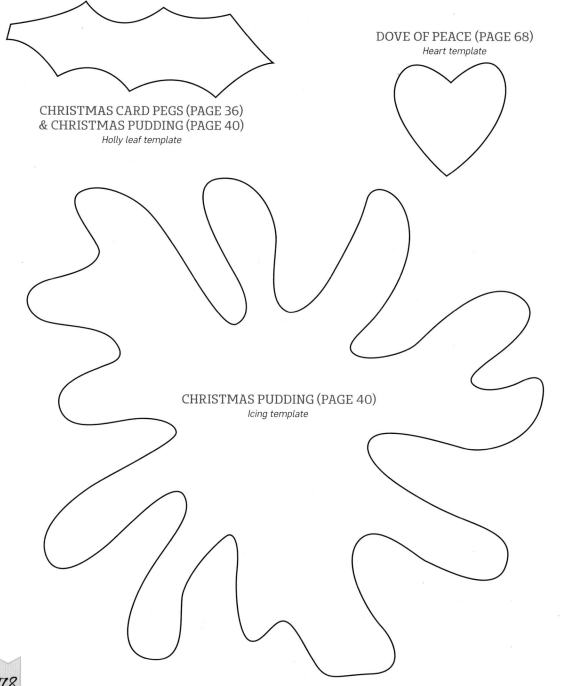

**CHRISTMAS CARD PEGS (PAGE 36)
& CHRISTMAS PUDDING (PAGE 40)**
Holly leaf template

DOVE OF PEACE (PAGE 68)
Heart template

CHRISTMAS PUDDING (PAGE 40)
Icing template

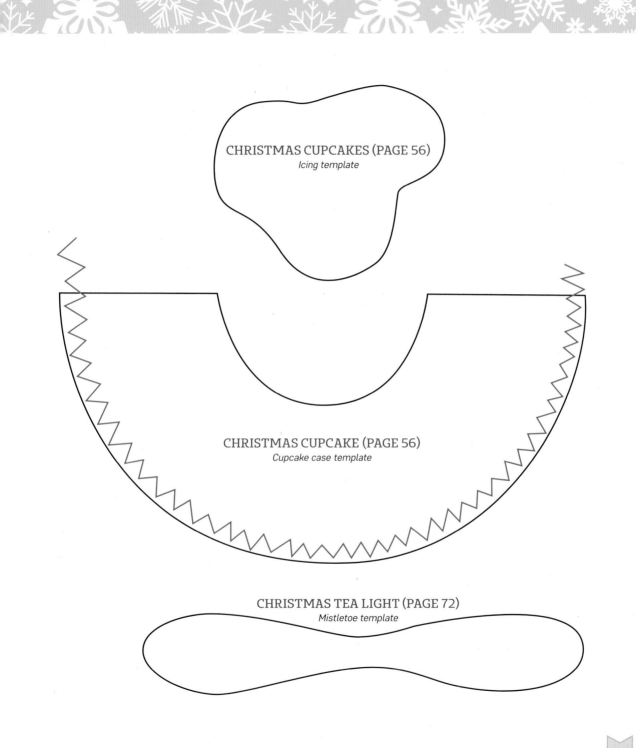

CHRISTMAS CUPCAKES (PAGE 56)
Icing template

CHRISTMAS CUPCAKE (PAGE 56)
Cupcake case template

CHRISTMAS TEA LIGHT (PAGE 72)
Mistletoe template

Acknowledgements

I would like to thank the team at
Search Press, including May Corfield for her
editorial support; photographers Laura Forrest,
Ruth Jenkinson, and Paul Bricknell for their
beautiful photography; and Marrianne Miall and
Juan Hayward for the lovely design work.
Also, a special thank you to everyone supporting
me by buying a copy of my Christmas book –
I hope you enjoy it!